INCREASING EMPLOYEE PRODUCTIVITY

An Introduction To Value Management

Lynn Tylczak

CRISP PUBLICATIONS, INC.
Los Altos, California

INCREASING EMPLOYEE PRODUCTIVITY
An Introduction To Value Management

Lynn Tylczak

CREDITS
Editor: **Tony Hicks**
Designer: **Carol Harris**
Typesetting: **Interface Studio**
Cover Design: **Carol Harris**
Artwork: **Ralph Mapson**

Copyright © 1990 by Crisp Publications, Inc.
Printed in the United States of America

Crisp books are distributed in Canada by Reid Publishing, Ltd., P.O. Box 7267, Oakville, Ontario, Canada L6J 6L6.

In Australia by Career Builders, P.O. Box 1051, Springwood, Brisbane, Queensland, Australia 4127.

And in New Zealand by Career Builders, P.O. Box 571, Manurewa, New Zealand.

Library of Congress Catalog Card Number 89-81244
Tylczak, Lynn
Increasing Employee Productivity
ISBN 1-56052-010-8

PREFACE

Managers who look to purchase the best in goods and services must keep an eye on the bottom line. Since seeing is believing, they may be blinded to all but the most visible business ratio: Return On Investment (ROI).

But everyday ROI figures are Rarely Of Importance in the long run. They are too shortsighted for the farseeing manager. Consider training costs or research and development expenditures. Both are current expenses that may not affect the assets column of the balance sheet for months to come. What does that time lag do to ROI? It skews the facts and figures, making them a Rendition Of Imbalances.

The ROI that offers managers their greatest profit payback is this: Return On Ingenuity. It requires the proper work environment, a strong employee suggestion program, employee training and assistance, and a positive attitude.

This book will help you create all four. You'll learn:

- The power of employee suggestions

- How to create an environment that encourages creativity

- A step-by-step process that employees can use to identify, analyze, and refine profitable ideas

- How to turn apathetic automatons into tinkerers and "thinker-ers."

So ROI: Read On For Illumination!

Lynn Tylczak

Lynn Tylczak

ACKNOWLEDGMENTS

It is not enough to acknowledge the individuals who have provided the research for this book. It is also important to recognize their successes. Among those people:

> John Maurer, PE, CVS, Productivity and Quality Center, Westinghouse, Pittsburgh, PA
>
> Gary Robinson, Boeing Company, Seattle, WA
>
> Thomas R. Chamberland, PE, CVS, U. S. Army Corps of Engineers, San Francisco, CA
>
> Pete Megani, CVS, Martin Marietta Orlando Aerospace, Orlando, FL

Typical organization success stories:

> Westinghouse discovers that replacing a rectangular transfer tank with a similar-size cylinder would be more efficient and save $350,000 annually.
>
> A major defense contractor improves a jet's braking system by adding a simple spacer. Brake life increases from 700 hours to 1229 hours and savings total $38.3 million.
>
> The Army Corps of Engineers spends $40,000 on its Heppner, Oregon, Value Management study. Total savings: $11.6 million. Cost to savings ratio: 1 to 290.

This book is also dedicated to:

> Joseph, Erik and Lesley Tylczak for their inspiration and motivation
>
> and to:
>
> Arthur E. Mudge, CVS, Value Associates, Bethel Park, Pennsylvania. Though not the "father" of Value Management he is certainly its shining sun!

ABOUT THIS BOOK

This book is two for the price of one. It tells you about successful suggestion programs and about Value Management (VM)—a double promise of success for the businessperson who puts its guidelines into practice.

Section I shows how involving employees in Value Management can—correction, WILL— save money while improving quality, productivity, and morale. VM is working for more than half the ''In Search of Excellence'' companies. It will work for yours.

Section II looks at the requirements for a successful employee suggestion program. Are you doing everything necessary to make your program a winner? HINT: Money isn't everything. Many successful suggestion programs could be financed out of petty cash!

Section III introduces VM—a little-known technique used by top companies to help employees find new ways to achieve more (quality, productivity, service) at less cost. These Value Management methods can be applied by virtually any employee to virtually any problem with a virtual guarantee of success.

Section IV is Value Management in action, a real-world case study of how VM helped a typist increase her department's productivity on one business form by over 800 percent.

Any company can increase quality while cutting costs—because any company can implement Value Management (the method) and a successful suggestion program (the vehicle). Thanks to the information in this book, you're only 50 minutes away!

CONTENTS

SECTION *I*

WHAT'S IN IT FOR ME?

THE POWER OF SUGGESTIONS

In the late 1800s, Lister and Company was Britain's leading silk supplier. Its incredible profits set the standard for corporate fashion and overindulgence. One mill was so large that a car could have been driven around the top of its chimney.

In 1912 a Lister employee, scientist/chemist Samuel Courtauld, showed management a new synthetic silk he had created. He called it "rayon."

Lister management tore the ragamuffin's idea to shreds, saying that the public would *insist* on real silk. So poor Samuel Courtauld had to go out on his own to create—and profit from—a multibillion dollar industry.

Can a good employee suggestion program really turn an innovative sow's ear into a silk purse—one that will keep paying dividends far into the future?

There are no guarantees. But there are some certainties. In the next few pages, you'll see what a well-designed and well-administered employee suggestion program can do for you. It offers smart front-line managers the opportunity to move their department ahead on all fronts.

DON'T CLOSE YOURSELF OFF
TO EMPLOYEE SUGGESTIONS

DESIRED CHANGES

If you aren't completely sold on the idea of beefing up your employee suggestion program, consider the benefits you'll be buying into.

Take a few minutes. List *all* of the things you would like to improve in your business. Think big: people, products, profits, procedures, processes, whatever.

I'd like to improve:

_____

_____

_____

_____

_____

_____

_____

_____

_____

_____

_____

_____

_____

_____

TRANSPIRED CHANGES

Match your desired changes to the "transpired changes" listed below. Chances are, your entire wish list appears below—plus a few other ideas you wish you'd listed.

These transpired changes are improvements documented by top International companies (Honeywell, IBM, Martin Marietta, Westinghouse, to name a few) as a result of internal Value Management employee suggestion programs.*

Transpired changes:

- *Cost improvements and other money matters*—Substantial cost savings, improved cash flow, elimination of unnecessary or costly items

- *Quality corrections*—Higher quality products or services, better quality control

- *Progress in products or services*—Substantial improvements in product competitiveness, performance, reliability, packaging, and weight

- *Improved procedures or processes*—Streamlined internal logistics, shorter production lead time, improved parts availability

- *Personnel pluses*—Increased leadership qualities, better teamwork, improved communications, higher productivity, more work force creativity, greater acceptance and use of new ideas and technology, higher morale, lower turnover rates

Think about your "desired changes" again, (page 3). If you'd like to add another wish—that you, too, had a VM-based employee suggestion program—your wish is our command. In the following chapters you'll learn how to put VM to work for you.

*Source: Society of American Value Engineers, *Value Program Survey*

THE VALUE OF EMPLOYEE INPUT

Focusing on changes inspired by employees rather than managers offers another bevy of benefits:

- Employees often have a better feel than managers for how procedures and processes could be improved.

  Familiarity with the job doesn't breed contempt. It breeds creativity ("How would I do this if it were up to me? How could I make my job easier?"). Hands-on experience creates an awareness of opportunities and problems that isn't always shared by hands-off managers.

- Employees may have a more diverse background than managers.

  Hourly workers are more transient than managers. Ideas picked up on other jobs can be a great pick-me-up for problem areas ("Where I used to work we solved that by.... We used to....").

- Employees can experiment without upsetting the applecart.

  Employees can tinker with a new idea and generate very little attention. Managers, investigating the same procedure, would create concern.

- Employee-based ideas fare better in the unfair game of politics.

  Which ideas get a better reception from the work force: proposals from peers or management-mandated manifestos? You got it!

- Employee suggestion programs strengthen important organizational dynamics.

  You can't do all the work yourself. You have to delegate. A sound employee suggestion program will facilitate—rather than debilitate—your efforts.

SECTION *II*

COMPONENTS OF A SUCCESSFUL SUGGESTION SYSTEM

THE THREE COMPONENTS

Like a three-legged stool, a successful employee suggestion program has three important "support systems." Programs without these basic components—Visibility, Ego Builders, and Structure—don't have a leg to stand on.

Building a profitable program is relatively easy. The fifty strategies that follow are a good place to start. For each item, ask yourself:

- Does our company use this tactic?
- If not, why not? Is it appropriate for us?
- Could we adapt it to fit our specific needs and circumstances?
- Do I have the authority to implement it? If not, who does?
- When could we start doing this?
- Who would handle any related administrative tasks?

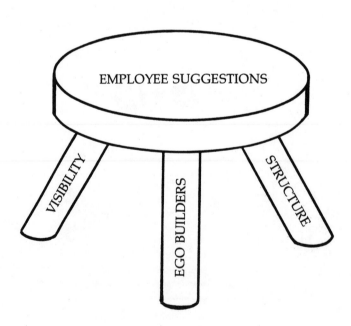

COMPONENT #1: VISIBILITY

The value of visibility is obvious. Out of sight, out of mind. Here are a few tactics to help employees keep their eyes on potential payoffs and their minds on innovative improvements.

	On My Authority	Needs Additional Authority	When Can We Start?
1. Reward suggestions with framed certificates			
2. Post accepted suggestions on the office bulletin board			
3. Post accepted suggestions in the lobby			
4. Post employee photos with their suggestions (people often know faces, but not names)			
5. Distribute congratulatory flyers			
6. Utilize a ''traveling trophy''			
7. Let participants use a specially designated parking space			
8. Acknowledge suggestions on an outside billboard, marquee, or readerboard			
9. Acknowledge suggestions over the PA system			
10. Acknowledge suggestions at regular meetings			
11. Congratulate the employee personally and publicly			
12. Acknowledge past suggestions in speeches, memos, training programs			
13. Mail a press release about significant suggestions to the workers' alumni association			
14. Mail a press release about significant suggestions to the local newspaper			
15. Mail a press release about major suggestions to appropriate trade journals or vendors			
16. Write an article about significant suggestions and route it to your firm's newsletter (even better, get it included in the quarterly corporate report)			
17. Use the employee and his or her suggestion in company advertising			

COMPONENT #2: EGO BUILDERS

There's an old country saying: ''You attract more flies with honey than with vinegar.'' The same holds true for your employee suggestion system. If a worker's experience with your program leaves a good taste in his or her mouth, he or she will come back for seconds.

These personal payoffs will help you reward employees (not necessarily with money!) for a job well done.

	On My Authority	Needs Additional Authority	When Can We Start?
18. Write a personal letter to the employee thanking him or her for the suggestion			
19. Write a personal letter to his or her family, recognizing the employee's input			
20. Write a letter to *your* boss, acknowledging the employee's success			
21. Write a letter to the employee's personnel file, acknowledging his or her idea (particularly important to promotion-conscious people)			
22. Have the *top* boss write a letter of congratulation			
23. Write a thank-you note to the employee on personal—*not company*—stationery			
24. Express personal admiration			
25. Voice your appreciation on a continuing basis			
26. Mention the worker's contribution at his or hers regularly scheduled employee review			
27. Consider—but don't feel bound to offer—monetary rewards			

COMPONENT #3: STRUCTURE

The only way to avoid a snafu system is to institute a PLAN—a Program Linking Administrative Needs. Here are a few helpful hints.

	On My Authority	Needs Additional Authority	When Can We Start?
28. Insure that the program is sensitive to people: their feelings, values, needs			
29. Help employees generate ideas (for example: suggest areas for improvement, demonstrate how past ideas can be adapted to newer needs)			
30. Help with any necessary research			
31. Train employees to spot potential improvements			
32. Encourage team efforts and suggestions			
33. Facilitate interdepartmental brainstorming			
34. Make the forms easy to use			
35. Develop easy-to-understand procedures and rules			
36. Make the program easy to access physically (readily available forms, drop boxes for completed forms)			
37. Have a self-replicating form			
38. Use a professional-looking form that employees will take seriously			

12

COMPONENT #3: STRUCTURE
(Continued)

	On My Authority	Needs Additional Authority	When Can We Start?
39. Number the suggestion forms to emphasize their importance			
40. Empower a formal and ongoing suggestion committee			
41. Make sure that each suggestion has a designated committee "champion"			
42. Make sure that each suggestion gets a formal and fair review, no shortcuts			
43. Keep employees advised on the progress of their idea(s)			
44. Set deadlines for committee decisions			
45. Make sure that employees are told why their idea was, or was not, accepted			
46. Allow employees to adapt suggestions when appropriate			
47. Make sure that internal promotion forms include a space to note program participation			
48. Make sure that employee review forms include a space to note program participation			
49. Commemorate employee suggestions in an ongoing photo album			
AND MOST IMPORTANT:			
50. DEMONSTRATE SERIOUS AND ONGOING TOP MANAGEMENT SUPPORT			

SELLING THE SUPPORT SYSTEMS

Visibility, ego builders, and structure will sell a suggestion program to your workers. Convincing other managers to buy into the program takes an entirely different sales pitch.

The key to success: managers aren't interested in how a program *works*, they are interested in *what it can do.* For example:

The Benefits of Visibility:

- A positive corporate image (we encourage innovation)
- A tighter focus on quality and cost goals
- Positive reinforcement for employees

The Benefits of Ego Builders:

- Increased worker confidence
- Greater loyalty and commitment to the company
- Motivated employees

The Benefits of Structure:

- Predictability (even in the midst of change)
- Confidence in ''the system''
- Continuity (this is no fadeable fad)

ARE YOU A SUGGESTION SABOTEUR?

Listed below are some of the telltale signs of the suggestion saboteur. Try not to be a "yes man" in any of these areas!

Yes	No	
_____	_____	I tend to defend the corporate status quo. To do otherwise would be disloyal.
_____	_____	I am often sceptical about change. "If it ain't broke (or broken badly!) don't fix it."
_____	_____	I remember people's failures. Loudly.
_____	_____	I forget people's successes. Quickly.
_____	_____	I don't question the ways things are done—they are obviously done that way for a reason!
_____	_____	I get irritated when employees ask "stupid" questions.*
_____	_____	I discourage employee input. If my subordinates really knew what they were talking about, they would be managers.
_____	_____	I sometimes take credit for ideas proposed by my subordinates.
_____	_____	I procrastinate. Even good employee suggestions sometimes wait around until I can get around to them.
_____	_____	I don't pay enough attention to the implementation of ideas. Things often slip through the cracks.
_____	_____	I think that wanting to change the status quo is really a covert or unconscious complaint.
_____	_____	When employees question the way things are done, I see the situation as being us (management) versus them (employees).
_____	_____	I believe I know more about the workings of the department than the employees. If there were changes that needed to be made, I would be the one to recognize them.
_____	_____	I wish employees would stop trying to tinker with the system and just do their work!

*There is no such thing as a stupid question—only stupid mistakes!

SECTION III

AN INTRODUCTION TO VALUE MANAGEMENT

SETTING UP THE PROCESS

Visibility, ego builders, and structure are the backbone of a good employee suggestion program. Value Management provides the muscle.

DEFINITION

Value Management is a step-by-step creative process that revolves around the word—FUNCTION. It helps employees identify better ways to provide necessary critical change.

Value Management, which was created and refined at General Electric, has an impressive 40-year track record. Many top companies—such as Boeing, Westinghouse, Black & Decker, General Dynamics—use VM to improve their product or service while cutting costs. When you use VM your company is in good company.

THE VM GROUND RULES

When you're breaking ground on a VM suggestion program, it is important to establish some ground rules.

GROUND RULE 1: Don't think of VM as simple cost cutting.

Focusing on costs alone results in shoddy products, slower service, and lower morale. It alienates customers and drives away business. VM *always* considers ''what you pay'' (costs) *and* ''what you get in return'' (quality). Employees should also be encouraged to submit ideas that *increase* costs, as long as there's an even greater increase in quality.

GROUND RULE 2: Listen for sour grapes via the grapevine.

Do your employees say things like the following?

- So-and-so isn't going to like this.
- Forget it—it's not my job!
- Maybe someday.
- What's wrong with the way we do it now?
- Oh, brother.
- What's he trying to prove?
- That's too much of a risk.
- We don't have the money to waste on that.
- Why bother?

If so, your program isn't doing its job. It hasn't answered the universal question: ''What's in it for me?''

THE VM GROUND RULES
(Continued)

GROUND RULE 3: Give employees directions rather than directives.

Steer employees toward successful suggestions. Encourage them to look for parts of their job that are:

- More complicated than necessary
- Frustrating (Things are often frustrating because they are poorly designed)
- Possible to change and fix
- Nonstandard or unique to your company (Do your competitors do it differently because they know something you don't?)

Teach employees to ask the acid tests of value:

- Does this product/component/task add value?
- Is it worth what it costs ($1 worth of use for $1 in costs)?
- Are all of its features required?
- Can anything else do what needs to be done?
- Are other companies paying less for the item? Could we?
- Can it be made or completed in a less expensive way?
- Are we using the right ''tools'' (technology, parts, training)?

GROUND RULE 4: Empower your employees.

Give your employees basic empowerment tools:

- Access to information
- The right to challenge old ideas
- The freedom to ask ''stupid'' questions (There are no stupid questions, only stupid mistakes.)
- Open lines of communication

THE SIX TASKS

Value Management involves six separate and important tasks.

TASK *1* *GATHER INFORMATION*

Collect the information needed to understand and analyze the product. (The same steps apply to any VM target: services, systems, processes, procedures.)

TASK *2* *IDENTIFY FUNCTIONS*

Define the product: not what it *is*, but what it *does*.

> **NOTE:** This step is what separates VM from all other analytical techniques. Other approaches search for incremental improvements. VM's functional focus allows employees to address more basic—and much more profitable—issues.

TASK *3* *GENERATE IDEAS*

Identify new ways to provide the required functions.

TASK *4* *CONSOLIDATE IDEAS*

Analyze the ideas and group the best ones into a few possible new products.

THE SIX TASKS (Continued)

TASK **5** *EVALUATE ALTERNATIVES*

Identify the combination of ideas that provide all of the required functions at the lowest cost.

TASK **6** *RECOMMEND THE IDEA*

Submit the best idea to the suggestion committee for review and action.

The following TASK pages should be passed on to employees. They will provide the basic VM guidance and framework for profitable employee suggestions.

Why a TASK format? Simply To Access and Stimulate "Kreativity!"

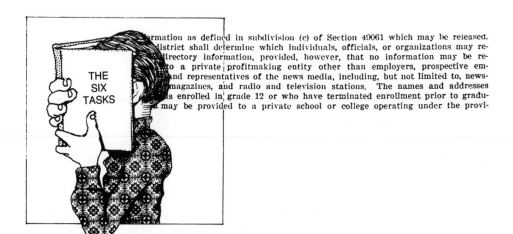

VALUE MANAGEMENT PRACTITIONERS

If VM sounds like a lot of work, you've got acute hearing. Still, VM pays its way.
If you ever need inspiration, refer to the following partial list of corporate
practitioners. It reads like a who's who of what's happening.

AM International
Allis Chalmers
B F Goodrich
Bell & Howell
Bendix
Black and Decker
Boeing Company
Borg Warner
Brunswick Corporation
CH2M Hill
Caterpillar Tractor
Control Data
Cummings Engine
Data General
Digital Equipment
Eaton
Ford Motor Company
Freightliner Corporation
General Dynamics
General Electric
Hewlett-Packard
Honeywell
Hughes Aircraft Company
IBM
Ingersoll Rand

John Deere
Lockheed
Mack Trucks
Martin Marietta
McKinsey & Company
Morton Thiokol
NCR Corporation
Nastar
Owens-Corning Fiberglass
Philips Industries
Playskool
RCA
Raytheon Company
Rockwell Corporation
St. Regis Paper
Smith & Wesson
Stanley Tools
Stouffers
Sunbeam Corporation
TRW
Tektronix
Teledyne Water Pik
Union Carbide
Westinghouse

SECTION *IV*

THE VM TASKS

GETTING FIT FOR VM TASKS

TASK 1 - GATHER INFORMATION

> Goal: To gather all the information needed to understand—and eventually analyze—the product in question.

Write a narrative about the product. Imagine you're describing it to someone who has never seen it—or anything like it—before. What would he or she need to know?

Answer such questions as: What is the product? What does it consist of? How does it work? What does it do? Does it do what it is supposed to do? What kind of track record does it have? What does it do well? Where does it fall short? What do people like or dislike about the product? What does it cost to produce (labor, materials, overhead)?

The amount of detail required will depend on the product. Add as many pages as you need.

NARRATIVE

_____

_____

_____

_____

_____

_____

_____

_____

_____

_____

_____

TASK 2 - IDENTIFY FUNCTIONS

> Goal: To completely define the product in terms of what it *does* and what it *must do*.

Fill in the Product Functions chart on the next page, using the following guidelines:

- **STEP 1 - DESCRIBE THE PRODUCT THROUGH ITS FUNCTIONS**

  List *everything* that the product does. Use only two words per function, a noun and a verb. For example, when used by a person, a pen *draws lines, writes letters, holds ink, prevents leaks,* and so on. If you can't describe a function in two words, break it into subfunctions. For example, the retractable tip function of a ballpoint pen could be described as ''tip can be retracted when not in use''— but that takes too many words. Break it down into two functions: *retracts tip, extends tip.*

- **STEP 2 - PRIORITIZE THE FUNCTIONS**

  Every product has one primary function (what it MUST do) and numerous secondary functions (extras). Rank the functions that you've listed: 1 for the primary function; 2 for the most important secondary function, and so on.

- **STEP 3 - CATEGORIZE THE FUNCTIONS**

  There are two types of functions: work functions and sell functions. Work functions are what make the product work. They are described by concrete verbs and measurable nouns (for example, *draws lines.)* Sell functions are what make the product saleable. They are described by abstract verbs and unmeasurable nouns (for example, *increases prestige).* Go through your list of functions and mark the work functions with W and the sell functions with S.

TASK *2* - *IDENTIFY FUNCTIONS*
(Continued)

PRODUCT FUNCTIONS

STEP 1 FUNCTION		STEP 2 PRIORITY	STEP 3 CATEGORY
VERB	NOUN	RANK	WORK OR SELL

A FUNCTIONAL EXAMPLE

Functional analysis is more difficult than it sounds. It's critical to get down to basics. Consider the following example.

The product: a gold-plated pen with corporate logo.

STEP 1 - DESCRIBE THE PRODUCT THROUGH ITS FUNCTIONS

What does this pen do? What functions does it provide? It:
draws lines, writes letters, holds ink, prevents leaks, retracts tip, extends tip, prevents evaporation, increases prestige, provides advertising.

STEP 2 - PRIORITIZE THE FUNCTIONS

What is the primary thing that the pen MUST do?
That depends. If the pen is meant to be used regularly, its primary function is *draws lines* or *writes letters*. If it was designed strictly to be a showpiece award, its primary function is *increases prestige*. Let's assume the pen will be used regularly for writing.

STEP 3 - CATEGORIZE THE FUNCTIONS

What must the pen do in order to work? It must:
draw lines, write letters, hold ink, prevent leaks, retract tip, extend tip, prevent evaporation.

What must the pen do in order to sell? It must:
increase prestige, provide advertising.

A FUNCTIONAL EXAMPLE (Continued)

The Product Functions chart for the gold-plated pen with corporate logo (page 27) would look something like this:

PRODUCT FUNCTIONS

STEP 1 FUNCTION		STEP 2 PRIORITY	STEP 3 CATEGORY
VERB	NOUN	RANK	WORK OR SELL
draws	lines	1	W
writes	letters	1	W
holds	ink	2	W
prevents	leaks	3	W
extends	tip	5	W
retracts	tip	6	W
prevents	evaporation	4	W
increases	prestige	8	S
provides	advertising	7	S

FUNCTIONAL FAUX PAS

Identifying these functional faux pas can lead to significant savings:

- ## Unnecessary work functions

  Work functions that don't increase the product's usefulness are unnecessary functions. Unnecessary functions waste money.

  > **Example:** The pen may conduct electricity, but that isn't important to penmanship. If the company is paying more for this work function, it is wasting money.

- ## Unnecessary sell functions

  Sell functions that don't affect the product's saleability are also unnecessary functions that waste money.

  > **Example:** The pen is gold plated to increase prestige. However, *unseen* gold plating on the inside would be a waste of money.

- ## Budget-busting functions

  Functions that cost more than they are worth, waste money.

  > **Example:** Salespeople could be given solid gold pens with the company logo. Such pens would certainly be prestigious, but the cost would be ridiculous.

TASK 3 - GENERATE IDEAS

> Goal: To identify new ways to provide the required functions.

TASK 3 will generate a long list of different ways to provide the product's necessary functions.

This is easier than it sounds because the immediate goal is idea quantity, not quality. TASK 3 primes the creative pump; it doesn't gum it up with premature judgments, ridicule, or censorship. Ideas are expected to run the gamut from sensational to silly.

The creative process goes like this:

- Ask the general questions on pages 37 through 39 to get things rolling.
- Use copies of pages 40 through 46 for each function. Label each page Function 1, Function 2, and so on.
- Ask the questions and/or apply the techniques as appropriate.
- Write down any ideas that come to mind, then quickly go on. Don't stop to think—that will mean you've stopped thinking!

The end result will be a comprehensive list of alternatives, both wacky and workable. In short, a place to start.

GETTING STARTED

Asking these general questions is a good way to unplug the creative cork.

Product Particulars

• What can be learned from analyzing what the product isn't?

_____

_____

_____

• What are the benefits and advantages of this product?

_____

_____

_____

• What are the drawbacks or disadvantages of this product?

_____

_____

_____

• Can one component be reworked to provide additional functions?

_____

_____

_____

• Can one function be split among several components?

_____

_____

_____

Personal Preferences

- If I were designing this thing from scratch, is this how I would provide the necessary functions? What would I have done instead?

  _____

  _____

  _____

- What don't I like about the product? Is anything a hassle?

  _____

  _____

  _____

Competitive Questions

- How do our competitors provide similar functions?

  _____

  _____

  _____

- Do our competitors provide better functions (less expensive, more reliable, more attractive)?

  _____

  _____

  _____

- How do we and our products differ from the competition?

  _____

  _____

  _____

COMPETITIVE QUESTIONS
(Continued)

- What is better, or worse, about competitors' products?

  _____

  _____

  _____

- What positive comments do customers make about competitors' products?

  _____

  _____

  _____

- Why do we lose customers to the competition?

  _____

  _____

  _____

THE FUNCTIONAL BASICS

FUNCTION #

- Is this function necessary? Could it be eliminated?

_____

_____

- How important is it?

_____

_____

- Is there a different or better way to provide it? For example?

_____

_____

_____

- Would adding this function give the product more value?

_____

_____

- Would increasing this function give the product more value?

_____

- Would decreasing this function give the product more value?

_____

- Would subtracting this function give the product more value?

_____

FUNCTION #

What changes might improve the product? It might be possible to:

Make it longer _____

Make it shorter _____

Make it bigger _____

Make it smaller _____

Make it stronger _____

Make it weaker _____

Make it thicker _____

Make it thinner _____

Make it more expensive (designer) _____

Make it cheaper _____

Make it hot _____

Make it cold _____

Make it one piece _____

Make it multipiece _____

Make it disposable _____

Make it reusable _____

THE FUNCTIONAL BASICS
(Continued)

It might be possible to:

Make it centralized _____

Make it decentralized _____

Make it faster _____

Make it slower _____

Make it simpler _____

Make it more complex _____

Make it softer _____

Make it harder _____

Make it rough _____

Make it smooth _____

Change its shape _____

Change its direction _____

Change its orientation _____

Change its positioning _____

Merge its pieces _____

Converge its pieces _____

Stratify its pieces _____

Combine its pieces _____

It might be possible to:

Redefine its character _____

Substitute parts _____

Interchange parts _____

Upgrade parts _____

Replace parts _____

Standardize parts _____

Stabilize parts _____

Reverse something _____

Improve resilience _____

Use color _____

Change its form _____

Incorporate separate functions into the basic unit _____

Preform components _____

Conform _____

CREATIVITY BY THE NUMBERS

THE RULE OF 15

Pick one function from the chart on page 31. Write down 15 different ways (even impractical ones!) to provide that function.

Example: For the function *connect papers,* ideas might include staples, paper clips, sewing, bubble gum, welding torch, nuclear fusion.

FUNCTION #

Ways to provide this function:

1. _____

2. _____

3. _____

4. _____

5. _____

6. _____

7. _____

8. _____

9. _____

10. _____

11. _____

12. _____

13. _____

14. _____

15. _____

THE RULE OF 26

Take one function. Write down 26 ways to provide that function, one for each letter of the alphabet (don't worry if you miss a few letters, like x, y, or z). Check the dictionary for inspiration (A: abolish, absorb, accelerate, accent, etc.).

FUNCTION #

Ways to provide this function:

A	
B	
C	
D	
E	
F	
G	
H	
I	
J	
K	
L	
M	
N	
O	
P	
Q	
R	
S	
T	
U	
V	
W	
X	
Y	
Z	

"VERB"-ALIZING WORK FUNCTIONS

Forget the function's noun and concentrate only on the verb. Why? A two-word function like *attach tag* may generate only three ideas (tie, staple, clamp); an unrestricted verb, *attach*, will generate many more (freeze, Velcro, graft, suction...).

NOTE: This technique only works on work functions.

Verb: _____

Ways to provide this function:

1. _____

2. _____

3. _____

4. _____

5. _____

6. _____

7. _____

8. _____

9. _____

10. _____

11. _____

12. _____

13. _____

14. _____

15. _____

TASK 4 - CONSOLIDATE IDEAS

Goal: To group our creative ideas into a few workable alternatives.

STEP 1 - Analyze The Ideas

This is "judgment day." The ideas generated during TASK 3 need to be analyzed and judged. Some are simply impractical. Those that could be practical need to be assessed. Each idea brings along its own baggage of advantages and disadvantages.

It's important to identify these pros and cons up front.

On the first go around, use a pencil! This form will probably be revised again and again. . . .

FUNCTION #

Creative ideas to provide this function	Advantages of this idea	Disadvantages of this idea	Costs*

* Costs include labor, overhead, raw materials, components, tools, and equipment. Don't get overwhelmed. For simple projects, relative costs or common sense are enough (for example, if it takes twice as long to do it this way, the labor costs are double).

TASK 4 - CONSOLIDATE IDEAS
(Continued)

These pros and cons are not forever. Review and amend them with the following questions in mind. (Thank Goodness for the pencil!)

• Can this idea's advantages or impact be strengthened? How?

_____

_____

_____

• Can this idea's disadvantages be lessened? How?

_____

_____

_____

• Can this idea be combined with others to give more advantages or fewer disadvantages? How?

_____

_____

_____

STEP 2 - Combine The Ideas

The creative ideas for the separate functions need to be brought together. The following form makes it easy.

PRODUCT

FUNCTION #1	
1. Idea that best provides function #1 at the lowest cost	
FUNCTION #2	
2. Idea that best provides function #2 at the lowest cost AND has the best fit with idea #1	
FUNCTION #3	
3. Idea that best provides function #3 at the lowest cost AND has the best fit with ideas #1 and #2	
FUNCTION #4	
4. Idea that best provides function #4 at the lowest cost AND has the best fit with ideas #1, #2, and #3	

Yes, compromise is necessary! For example, cost concerns become more and more important as the function becomes less important—you want to pay as little as possible for unimportant functions. No one idea will perfectly fulfill a function, fit with other ideas, and have the lowest cost—but one will probably come closer than any of the others. The key question is: Which idea offers the best value?

Repeat this process using the second best idea for function #1, then using the third best idea. In this way you will come up with several potential products. These can then be compared and contrasted.

STEP 3 - Compare and Contrast

Use the following questions to compare and contrast the product alternatives.

• What are the advantages of each alternative?

Alternative #1 _____

Alternative #2 _____

Alternative #3 _____

• What are the disadvantages?

Alternative #1 _____

Alternative #2 _____

Alternative #3 _____

• Do the advantages outweigh the disadvantages?

Alternative #1 _____

Alternative #2 _____

Alternative #3 _____

• What tradeoffs are involved?

Alternative #1 _____

Alternative #2 _____

Alternative #3 _____

• Can disadvantages be turned into solvable problems or advantages?

Alternative #1 _____

Alternative #2 _____

Alternative #3 _____

• Do the advantages of any alternative justify a change to the existing product?

_____

_____

_____

COMPARE AND CONTRAST
(Continued)

- Which alternative is the best? For what reasons—and by how much of a margin?

  Best _____

  Second best _____

  Third best _____

- How are the alternatives similar?

  _____

  _____

  _____

- How do the alternatives differ?

  _____

  _____

  _____

- Can alternatives be combined or adjusted to create a better option?

  _____

  _____

  _____

REWARDING RESOURCES

The following publications offer a wide variety of information on a wide variety of business subjects. Check with corporate, university, or public librarians. Publications that are not available on site are often available through interlibrary loan.

Publication	Helps you locate
Abridged Reader's Guide	General information
American Doctoral Dissertations	Business-oriented dissertations
American Library Directory	Specialized business libraries
Applied Science and Technology Index	Innovative ideas
Book Review Index	Books about specific business subjects
Books in Print	Books about specific business subjects
Business Periodicals Index	Magazine articles about specific business subjects
Directory of Special Libraries and Information Centers	Specialized collections of business writings
Dissertation Abstracts International	Business dissertations worldwide
Encyclopedia of Associations	Associations of experts in specialized business subjects
Gebbie House Magazine Directory	Corporate newsletters that can tell you how competitors do what you do
Guide to American Directories	Directories that can tell you where to find what you need to know

REWARDING RESOURCES
(Continued)

Publication	Helps you locate
Guide to Reference Books and The Guide to Reference Material	Help in using research materials
Industrial Arts Index	Magazine articles about industry
National Directory of Newsletters and Reporting Services	Newsletters that provide information on how competitors do what you do
National Trade and Professional Associations of the U.S.	Associations of experts in specialized business subjects
Thomas Register	Information on what's available from businesses
Ulrich's International Periodicals Directory	Magazines being published that cover specific business subjects

TASK 5 - EVALUATE ALTERNATIVES

> **Goal:** To gather all the information necessary to analyze—and judge—the alternative products.

TASK 5 is essentially an insurance policy. It insures that the alternative recommended will offer the best value—that it provides all of the functions with high quality at low cost.

Ask these four questions about each alternative:

• Should standard components be used?

> **Rationale:** Standard components tend to have a lower cost, better reputation, greater reliability, and easier availability than those made to order.

• Would a made-to-order component offer the best value?

> **Rationale:** New technologies or procedures may make special orders just what the innovator ordered.

• What do the experts think?

> **Rationale:** Check with peers, managers, vendors, customers, professional associations, trade journals, academics, and anyone else you can think of for feedback. They may have a different perspective, and may ask valid questions that you haven't thought of. Better late then never!

• Has the final idea had time to settle?

> **Rationale:** Waiting a week before submitting any idea will allow any last-minute inspirations to still be timely!

TASK 6 - RECOMMEND THE IDEA

> Goal: To present the idea to the suggestion committee in such a way that it will be accepted and implemented.

In some respects, TASK 6 is more important than any of its counterparts. Why? Because unless the idea is accepted and implemented, the first five tasks were a lost cause.

Here are some suggestions for dealing with suggestion committees:

- Learn about the committee members. Who are they? What do they like? What motivates them (primarily cost or quality)? Would they like to see your background material (the VM forms)?

- Always include cost information. Overestimate costs and underestimate savings. That way, any surprises will be good surprises.

- Go heavy on the facts and light on the guesstimates. Committee members can't dismiss relevant, verifiable, objective facts.

- Include before and after comparisons (costs, problems, opportunities, improvements so that committee members will understand the benefits of a suggestion.

- Show the how and why of any conclusions. Present the suggestion as a technical travelog.

- Stress the idea's benefits. What will the company gain by implementing it?

- Find a devil's advocate who will give the idea one devil of a time. If there's a serious wrinkle in the fabric of an idea the time to iron it out is before—not during—the committee presentation.

- If appropriate, suggest a timeline or strategy for implementation.

SECTION *V*

CASE STUDY

INTRODUCTION

The following is a real-world case study. It demonstrates how a successful employee suggestion program, teamed with viable VM, can yield unheard-of profits. In this case, productivity on a single business form increased by 800 percent, while error rates dropped from 68 percent to 2 percent. Morale and department turnover improved, and costs (recruitment, training, production, returns, corrections, mailing, materials) plummeted.

There's a lesson here on how employee suggestion and VM programs can lessen common management problems:

- They turn a problem situation into an opportunity.

- They facilitate the delegation of important tasks. Here the manager isn't just delegating a task, he or she is passing on the means to accomplish it.

- They allow managers to leverage their training efforts. Suggestion programs and VM guidelines are used again and again by motivated employees.

- They enhance teamwork (particularly between managers and employees). There is no us-versus-them, employees-versus-management mentality. The prevailing perspective becomes us versus it: employees AND managers versus the problem.

- They help managers transcend ''management'' and ascend to ''leadership.''

VM HELPS MANAGERS BECOME LEADERS

CASE STUDY
THE WC105 PROBLEM

"Great minds think alike," thought George when he heard complaints about form WC105 coming from the typing pool. WC105 had a bad reputation with typists. It was frustrating, difficult to type, and irritating to work with. Top typists considered themselves lucky to type 6 wpm on WC105. The department average on other forms was 52 wpm. No wonder it was the form everybody loved to hate.

George's perspective was different, but no less caustic. This form had the lowest productivity level of any in the company (only 10 words took 1 minute 39 seconds to type!). It created low morale and low quality standards (it had an incredible 68 percent error rate), high turnover, and high costs.

Clearly, something had to be done, but nobody was thinking clearly. George decided to help Miriam, an experienced and innovative employee, solve the paper problem by using VM.

Write what you think George should do in the space provided below. Then compare your answer with that of the author on page 54.

_____

_____

_____

_____

_____

_____

_____

_____

_____

CASE STUDY

GEORGE'S PLAN OF ACTION

The following is what George decided to do to help Miriam apply VM techniques to the problem.

- Help Miriam spot the potential for improvement.

  WC105 is frustrating to type because it is poorly designed. That makes it an excellent candidate for the suggestion program.

- Stress the benefits.

  What are the benefits Miriam will gain by participating in the suggestion program? Personal recognition, improved productivity, less stressful work, maybe financial compensation. . . .

- Encourage Miriam to use the VM process.

  VM won't just show Miriam where to start—it will tell her where to go. VM is her most direct route to the optimal option.

- Provide the necessary support.

  Give Miriam the resources she needs to fully analyze the form (VM and general information, undisturbed blocks of time, access to other departments). Help her identify potential pitfalls (both practical and political). Be there with moral and managerial support (including feedback, encouragement, praise).

In short, facilitate, rather then debilitate, Miriam's efforts. That's what management—and Value Management—is all about.

CASE STUDY
A DETAILED SOLUTION

TASK *1*

> Goal: To gather all the information needed to understand—and eventually analyze—the product in question.

George's initial TASK 1 actions:

- Give Miriam the first VM form. (It's on page 29.) Discuss how to write a narrative and provide examples.

- Acknowledge problems with WC105. Stress Miriam's right to ask any questions she sees fit.

- Answer any questions Miriam might have about the suggestion program or the VM process. NOTE: Miriam will have little—if any—knowledge about the VM process. Suggest that she take each step as it comes rather then trying to get one step ahead.

Here's a summary of Miriam's findings:

WC105 is a form used on 5 percent of all new Workmen's Compensation policies. It consists of two similar pieces of paper (A and B). These are sheets of white 8½" by 11" paper, printed on the front and back. They look identical; the only difference is that A is printed on NCR paper. A and B are bound together at the top in such a way that they can be pulled apart. Copy A is for our use, copy B is for the clients. A copy of the form is attached.

Each sheet contains seven information blocks. The front sides contain an address block and three sections of client data. The backs contain three more client sections.

We type the address block. Some or all of the six client sections must be completed. We type Xs in front of those. We mail the form to the client, who completes it. He separates the two sheets. He keeps the second sheet for his records and sends us back the top copy.

CASE STUDY: TASK 1 (Continued)

The most we ever type is a client name and address and six Xs, yet the form takes an average of 1 minute 39 seconds to complete. This works out to an average typing speed of 6 words per minute. On our other departmental forms the average speed is 52 wpm.

Productivity is very low on WC105 because completing this form requires up to 26 steps:

Step 1	Insert the front side of the form.
Step 2	Align the paper.
Step 3	Type the client's name and address.
Step 4	Realign the paper.
Step 5	Type the first X.
Step 6	Realign the paper.
Step 7	Type the second X.
Step 8	Realign the paper.
Step 9	Type the third X.
Step 10	Remove the paper.

Thanks to NCR paper, steps 1–10 complete the front sides of sheets A and B. However, NCR paper doesn't work both ways. The backs of sheets A and B must be completed separately, while the two sheets remain bound together at the top.

Step 11	Insert the back side of sheet B.
Step 12	Align the paper.
Step 13	Type the fourth X.
Step 14	Realign the paper.
Step 15	Type the fifth X.
Step 16	Realign the paper.
Step 17	Type the sixth X.
Step 18	Remove the paper.

Now comes the hardest part:

Steps 19–26	Repeat steps 11–18 for the back of sheet A.

WC105 is universally disliked. Clients have a hard time filling it out properly and it often comes back incomplete. (For example, the client only fills out the back side on sheet B, then sends us back sheet A—with the back side not completed!) When this happens, we have to type another WC105 and resubmit it to the client, hoping he or she will fill it out correctly the second time.

George's follow-up TASK 1 actions:

- Discuss the narrative with Miriam. Provide feedback or insight by means of questions: Is there anything else you need to know? Doesn't there seem to be a lot of repetitive steps? Isn't there an awful lot of action for so little typing?

- Provide additional encouragement. Miriam has five more steps to go!

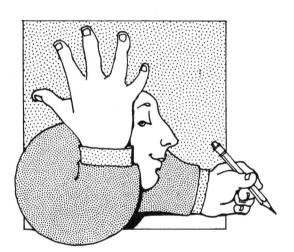

FIVE STEPS TO GO

CASE STUDY

Goal: To completely define the product in terms of what it *does* and what it *must do*.

George's initial TASK 2 actions:

- Give Miriam the second VM form. (The Product Functions form on page 31.) Discuss how it works and provide examples, if possible from a similar project.

- Stress the importance of taking VM one step at a time. This step seems so— well, *simplistic*—that it is often hurried through. Explain to Miriam that it's this step that makes the process so successful. So it's worth spending some time on.

- Complete the TASK 2 forms himself. Why? Spotting all the necessary product functions can be tricky, particularly on a first try. By compiling his own functional list, George can compare his conclusions with Miriam's. If necessary, he can suggest that Miriam consider additional functions. Not to second-guess Miriam, but to provide a backup. It's essential to cover all functions; missing some of them would cripple the VM's effectiveness and hinder Miriam's efforts.

Here's a summary of Miriam's findings:

WC105 has five functions:

collect information, instruct client, make copies, separate copies, categorize information.

CASE 2: TASK 2 (Continued)

The ranking:

    Priority #1 - collect information
    Priority #2 - categorize information
    Priority #3 - instruct client
    Priority #4 - make copies
    Priority #5 - separate copies

Work or sell functions:

    All are work functions

George's follow-up TASK 2 actions:

- Use feedback to help Miriam question the status quo. For example:

Does WC105's primary function—*collect information*—necessitate its own form? (Could this data be collected on the original insurance application, for example?)

Is enough being spent to provide the primary function? (Obviously not, when there's a 68 percent error rate!)

Are the two ''copy'' functions necessary (*make copies* and *separate copies*)? The copies are what complicate this form. Couldn't clients make photocopies, as they do on all other WC forms?

Steps 4–26 fulfill the *instruct client* function, by telling the client which sections to complete. Could we rearrange the instructions to the client so that 88 percent of our efforts are not wasted on secondary concerns?

Is it necessary to *categorize information*? Directing clients to categories requires a lot of effort. Couldn't clients simply be asked to complete all appropriate questions?

- Encourage Miriam not just to think, but to think BIG!

CASE STUDIES

TASK **3**

Goal: To identify new ways to provide the required functions.

George's initial TASK 3 actions:

- Give Miriam the appropriate VM forms. (Questions to Get the Ball Rolling, pages 37 through 39, the Functional Basics, pages 40–43, and Creativity by the Numbers, pages 44 through 46.) Discuss how these forms work and provide examples.

- Provide the necessary backup. TASK 3 can be long and frustrating. Follow Miriam's progress closely. Provide encouragement and subtle prompting. Assist with research and contacts.

Here's a summary of Miriam's creative ideas:

Function 1: *Collect information*

Is this the best way to collect information? Could we: Use the phone? Ask agents to submit the data when appropriate (either through an agent-based form or through a regular memo)? Add these questions to other forms (the original application form, other followup WC forms)? Mail all clients a generic WC105 form and ask them to fill out any applicable sections? Have a computer-generated form that includes only the sections necessary for that particular client?

Are we collecting information efficiently and effectively? Could we: Delete redundant or unnecessary data? Ask for more data (for example, three years' payroll records rather than just the most recent quarter's? Require a better class of data (for example, audited—rather than informal—financials)? Request comments (for example, if the answer is not positive, does the client have an explanation)? Utilize "exception" reporting? (Since the form only applies to 5 percent of all clients, and only 5 percent of returned forms will require further action, couldn't we ask clients to complete certain sections *only if such and such a condition exists?*)

Is this the best format for collecting information? Could we: Make this a one-sided form by using longer or wider paper, narrower margins, smaller type, less copy? Use carbon paper instead of NCR paper? (Flipping carbon paper is faster than retyping a page.) Use double-sided carbon paper? (Strategically placed "holes" in the carbon paper would allow typists to type the front sides simultaneously then flip the form over and type the back sides simultaneously.)

CASE STUDY: TASK 3 (Continued)

Function 2: *Categorize information*

Could we: Eliminate sections and simply ask clients to complete the applicable questions? Make each section a separate piece of paper and insert pages rather than type instructions (a process already used on endorsement sheets)? Align all columns vertically to eliminate realignments? Color-code sections for easy reference? Use fewer categories? Name the categories, rather than simply identifying them with generic Xs?

Function 3: *Instruct client*

Could we: Improve communications by using bigger print, clearer wording, colored type? Type all instructions in one place, replacing Xs with letters referring to the sections. (''Complete sections A and E'')? Write Xs by hand to eliminate typing?

Functions 4 and 5: *Make copies and separate copies*

Could we eliminate the copy function entirely and suggest that clients make their own photocopies? (NOTE: With the existing WC105, sheet B is not a legal copy of sheet A, since the back pages are actually typed separately.) Could we have clients complete a one-page WC105 form, then send it back to clients when we are finished with it (keeping a photocopy for our files, if desired)?

George's follow-up TASK 3 actions:

- Provide feedback without making negative judgments.

- Encourage Miriam to get ideas from other sources (peers, other departments, forms designers, managers, agents, clients, printers).

CASE STUDY

TASK **4**

Goal: To group our creative ideas into a few workable alternatives.

George's initial TASK 4 actions:

- Give Miriam the appropriate VM forms. (They're on pages 47–51.) Discuss how they work and provide examples.

- Remind Miriam that the alternatives she comes up with can be quite different from the current process. Encourage major overhauls. Major overhauls bring major improvements.

- Offer to help with feedback or refinements whenever necessary.

Here's a summary of Miriam's alternatives:

Alternative #1:
Eliminate WC105. Have agents add the information to an insurance application whenever necessary. This could be done via a new WC105 form or a regular memo.

Alternative #2:
Mail out a revised generic WC105 form to all new policyholders. Ask them to complete any applicable questions.

Alternative #3:
Redesign the form to fit on one side of a legal-size sheet of paper. Print all instructions on one area. Specify which lettered sections the client should complete ("Please complete sections A and E"). Eliminate sheet B; add a sentence to the instructions suggesting that the client make his own photocopy.

The new form's instructions would look something like those shown on the facing page.

CASE STUDY: TASK 4 (Continued)

Client's name and address: [NOTE: without the lines, which used to require paper alignment]

Please complete section(s):   and return the completed form to this office. Keep a photocopy of the form for your files.

Completing this form would require only 6 steps, instead of the current form's 26 steps.

Step 1	Insert the form.
Step 2	Align the paper.
Step 3	Type the client's name and address.
Step 4	Go to the space after the instruction "Please complete section(s)".
Step 5	Type the letters for the sections to be filled in (A, B, C, D, E, and/or F).
Step 6	Remove the paper.

Alternative #4:
Same as alternative #3, except a second page (a colored client copy) is attached. The top sheet would be a tear-off NCR sheet. Instruct the client to remove and keep the colored sheet.

George's follow-up TASK 4 actions:

• Help Miriam refine her alternatives. Add additional perspective and guidance about office politics, acceptability, costs.

• Offer evaluations (positive perspective) without being judgmental (negative perspective).

CASE STUDY

TASK **5**

> Goal: To gather all the information necessary to analyze—and judge—the alternative products.

George's initial TASK 5 actions:

- Encourage Miriam to give her alternatives another once-over as per TASK 5 guidelines.

- Facilitate the feedback process. Assist in soliciting ideas. Cushion harsh appraisals. Help interpret advice. Propose written feedback for possible submission to the suggestion committee.

These are Miriam's findings:

Standardized or made-to-order materials were not big factors in this study. However, expert feedback (from peers, manager, agents, clients) played a major role. For example:

Alternative #1, having agents collect this information when appropriate, was judged politically impractical. The company was trying desperately to improve the agents' productivity. Increase their workload? Not likely!

Alternative #2, developing a generic form and having clients answer any applicable questions, was more popular with the experts. But there was one nagging question. Would policyholders always know which questions were applicable? Alternative #2 could create more problems than it solved.

CASE STUDY: TASK 5 (Continued)

Alternative #3, designing a larger, one-page form, was very popular. Twenty production steps were eliminated. So was the copy, which turned out to be quite unnecessary. Miriam learned that 82 percent of all clients didn't keep a copy of the form. Those who did often made a photocopy—a legal copy—of the original form. Alternative #3 maximized the necessary functions and didn't waste time or money providing peripherals.

Alternative #4, adding a client copy to Alternative #3, was seen as functionally fine, but not as efficient as Alternative #3. The cost of providing a tear-off copy was seen as unnecessary.

Miriam decided to submit Alternative #3 to the suggestion committee.

George's follow-up TASK 5 actions:

- Review Miriam's information and conclusion. Ask questions and clarify.

- Note the quality of feedback received from the experts. George may wish to consult them again for future projects!

A VM SOLUTION IS IN SIGHT!

CASE STUDY

> Goal: To present the idea to the suggestion committee in such a way that it will be accepted and implemented.

George's initial TASK 6 actions:

- Discuss the presentation and the suggestion committee with Miriam. Answer any questions, address any fears.

- Help Miriam prepare her presentation. Act as a practice feedback-flinging "audience."

- Insure that Miriam has all the material and equipment she needs to make her formal presentation.

- Help Miriam secure a champion for her idea on the suggestion committee.

Miriam's presentation:

> Miriam dummies up a proposed Alternative #3 form. She submits it to the suggestion committee, along with her completed suggestion form and backup documentation (all the VM forms she has filled out along the way).
>
> On the day of the presentation, she and George arrive at the suggestion committee meeting with a typewriter, a dormant WC file, a WC105 form, an Alternative #3 form, and the backup documentation. Miriam's champion has already discussed her idea with the committee and given his own positive recommendation.
>
> Using information from the dormant WC file, Miriam completes a WC105 form. Elapsed time: 1 minute 45 seconds. Using the same dormant WC file, she completes an Alternative #3 form in 12 seconds. She explains how her alternative reduces typist errors and client errors. Clearly, her alternative is worth pursuing.
>
> She offers to answer any questions from the suggestion committee, but there are none. In fact, there is no opposition to her well-presented, well-documented alternative. The suggestion is unanimously accepted and implemented immediately.

George's follow-up TASK 6 action:

- Celebrate. Miriam's success is his success, too.

CASE STUDY

TASK **7**

TASK 7? *What* TASK 7?

True, Value Management only requires six TASKs. The following has nothing to do with Value Management and everything to do with plain old management. It is the checklist that George uses to insure that this one success fertilizes many future suggestions, both from Miriam and from the other typists.

**Check
When
Completed**

☐ Congratulate Miriam publicly and privately.

☐ Bring donuts for the entire department!

☐ Write the top boss a letter referencing Miriam's success.

☐ Draft a congratulatory letter for the top boss to sign and send to Miriam.

☐ Have the approval form from the suggestion committee framed for Miriam. Have the maintenance department hang it next to her desk.

☐ Send Miriam a letter of thanks and admiration on personal stationery.

☐ Enter Miriam's idea into the tickler file every three months as a reminder to say ''Thanks again.''

☐ Have Miriam demonstrate and explain the form to the other typists. Let her be ''queen for a day.''

☐ Talk with Miriam about her monetary reward (at this company, employees receive 5 percent of all savings resulting from an adopted suggestion, for a period of two years and up to a maximum of $10,000—a level that Miriam's idea easily reaches).

☐ Get a copy of the suggestion committee's comments—both for Miriam's benefit and for yours. What impresses them? What are they looking for? What part of the idea presentation had the most impact?

CASE STUDY: TASK 7 (Continued)

☐ Send a written thank you to all of the experts who provided feedback. Their help can be crucial in developing future ideas.

☐ Schedule a week on the outside readerboard for Miriam and her idea.

☐ Have Miriam's success announced over the office loudspeaker.

☐ Inform everyone involved on the outcome of the presentation. Everyone who played a part in creating or developing the idea is a part of the success story.

☐ Have Miriam's suggestion and her picture posted on the lunch room bulletin board.

☐ Have congratulatory flyers designed and printed. Distribute them widely—to co-workers in Miriam's department, people she works with in other departments, insurance agents in her region....

☐ Schedule Miriam for the "traveling trophy" and the "employee of the month" parking space.

☐ Start the next departmental meeting by recognizing Miriam and her idea.

☐ Route a "thank you" card around the department and have everybody sign it.

☐ Publicize Miriam's idea to various professionals around the company and encourage them to reference it in speeches, memos, training programs, the company newsletter, quarterly report, company advertising.

☐ Have Miriam's picture and a write-up of her idea entered in the corporate scrapbook.

☐ Distribute a press release about Miriam's success to her alumni association, the local newspaper, the agent's newsletter, insurance trade journals.

☐ Send a copy of Miriam's idea to the department that initially designed the form. Maybe they can learn something!

☐ Write a note for Miriam's files documenting her success.

☐ Have Miriam's suggestion and her picture posted out in the lobby.

☐ Ask Miriam and the other typists if there is anything else they would like to see changed. If they do, you have this great procedure called Value Management that....

SECTION *VI*

CONCLUSION

GO FOR IT!

We initially talked about ROI—Return On Investment—and how it was Rarely Of Importance to top managers in the long run.

It is clear that employee suggestion programs and Value Mangement are an entirely different story. Between them, a manager can reduce costs while improving product or service quality, productivity, morale, turnover, reliability, creativity, teamwork, and leadership.

The suggestion/VM program duo is one of the few partnerships in business that is truly a win-win situation. The only losers are those who don't get with the program!

SUGGESTION SYSTEMS IN A NUTSHELL

Good employee suggestion systems are not empty shell games. They require a solid structure. The system must be easy to access. Employees should know what to expect and should get what they expect. The program should be designed for ease of use and a minimum of tensions. In short, this profit-building program should be given the same businesslike attention as other profit centers.

Visibility is also critical to a successful program. Publicity pays. Promote the suggestion program and the employees who participate in it. Everybody wants their moment in the spotlight. By highlighting successful employee innovations, you not only let employees shine—you shine by reflected glory.

The ego builders built into a successful suggestion system are the building blocks for future success. These "strokes" enhance employee confidence and creativity. Employees with a higher level of self-esteem turn in a higher number of profitable ideas.

Strong employee suggestion systems are a means to an important end. Companies that treat their suggestion programs like an afterthought will not get what they're after.

VALUE MANAGEMENT IN A NUTSHELL

Value Management is a set of techniques that help employees identify creative ways to provide product or service functions. The steps are clear and concise:

1. Gather the information needed to analyze the product.

2. Define the product in terms of what it does and what it must do.

3. Identify new ways to provide these functions.

4. Group these ideas into a few workable alternatives.

5. Evaluate the proposed alternatives.

6. Recommend the best alternative.

However, the steps that management needs to take to make the suggestion work are less clear. It's important that you create a positive mind set. You must guide employees through the value process without making them feel hampered or pampered. Remember, you can give employees the tools to think, but they have to do the thinking.

The fifty minutes you invested in this book can reap a lifetime of benefits if you use these principles faithfully. Perhaps you will begin to think of ROI as Rewards Over Infinity!

ADDITIONAL SOURCES

For further information on employee suggestion programs, contact:

The National Association of Suggestion Systems (NASS)
230 N. Michigan Avenue, Suite 1200
Chicago, IL 60601
(312) 372-1770

For further information on Value Management, contact:

The Society of American Value Engineers (SAVE)
60 Revere Drive, Suite 500
Northbrook, IL 60062
(708) 480-1730

Companies interested in making a major commitment to VM, or those that wish to use VM on more complex projects, are strongly urged to get on-the-job guidance or training from a Certified Value Specialist (CVS). For a free referral to a CVS who works in your specific industry or geographic area, contact:

Specialized and Accredited Value Engineers Referral Service (SAVERS)
3504 Turner Road S.E.
Salem, OR 97302

NOTES

FOR OTHER FIFTY-MINUTE SELF-STUDY BOOKS
SEE ORDER FORM AT THE BACK OF THE BOOK.

NOTES

FOR OTHER FIFTY-MINUTE SELF-STUDY BOOKS
SEE ORDER FORM AT THE BACK OF THE BOOK.

NOTES

NOTES

FOR OTHER FIFTY-MINUTE SELF-STUDY BOOKS
SEE ORDER FORM AT THE BACK OF THE BOOK.

THE FIFTY-MINUTE SERIES

Quantity	Title	Code #	Price	Amount
	MANAGEMENT TRAINING			
	Self-Managing Teams	000-0	$7.95	
	Delegating For Results	008-6	$7.95	
	Successful Negotiation — Revised	09-2	$7.95	
	Increasing Employee Productivity	010-8	$7.95	
	Personal Performance Contracts — Revised	12-2	$7.95	
	Team Building — Revised	16-5	$7.95	
	Effective Meeting Skills	33-5	$7.95	
	An Honest Day's Work: Motivating Employees To Excel	39-4	$7.95	
	Managing Disagreement Constructively	41-6	$7.95	
	Training Managers To Train	43-2	$7.95	
	Learning To Lead	043-4	$7.95	
	The Fifty-Minute Supervisor — Revised	58-0	$7.95	
	Leadership Skills For Women	62-9	$7.95	
	Systematic Problem Solving & Decision Making	63-7	$7.95	
	Coaching & Counseling	68-8	$7.95	
	Ethics In Business	69-6	$7.95	
	Understanding Organizational Change	71-8	$7.95	
	Project Management	75-0	$7.95	
	Risk Taking	76-9	$7.95	
	Managing Organizational Change	80-7	$7.95	
	Working Together In A Multi-Cultural Organization	85-8	$7.95	
	Selecting And Working With Consultants	87-4	$7.95	
	PERSONNEL MANAGEMENT			
	Your First Thirty Days: A Professional Image in a New Job	003-5	$7.95	
	Office Management: A Guide To Productivity	005-1	$7.95	
	Men and Women: Partners at Work	009-4	$7.95	
	Effective Performance Appraisals — Revised	11-4	$7.95	
	Quality Interviewing — Revised	13-0	$7.95	
	Personal Counseling	14-9	$7.95	
	Attacking Absenteeism	042-6	$7.95	
	New Employee Orientation	46-7	$7.95	
	Professional Excellence For Secretaries	52-1	$7.95	
	Guide To Affirmative Action	54-8	$7.95	
	Writing A Human Resources Manual	70-X	$7.95	
	Winning at Human Relations	86-6	$7.95	
	WELLNESS			
	Mental Fitness	15-7	$7.95	
	Wellness in the Workplace	020-5	$7.95	
	Personal Wellness	021-3	$7.95	

THE FIFTY-MINUTE SERIES (Continued)

Quantity	Title	Code #	Price	Amount
	WELLNESS (CONTINUED)			
	Preventing Job Burnout	23-8	$7.95	
	Job Performance and Chemical Dependency	27-0	$7.95	
	Overcoming Anxiety	029-9	$7.95	
	Productivity at the Workstation	041-8	$7.95	
	COMMUNICATIONS			
	Technical Writing In The Corporate World	004-3	$7.95	
	Giving and Receiving Criticism	023-X	$7.95	
	Effective Presentation Skills	24-6	$7.95	
	Better Business Writing—Revised	25-4	$7.95	
	Business Etiquette And Professionalism	032-9	$7.95	
	The Business Of Listening	34-3	$7.95	
	Writing Fitness	35-1	$7.95	
	The Art Of Communicating	45-9	$7.95	
	Technical Presentation Skills	55-6	$7.95	
	Making Humor Work	61-0	$7.95	
	Visual Aids In Business	77-7	$7.95	
	Speed-Reading In Business	78-5	$7.95	
	Publicity Power	82-3	$7.95	
	Influencing Others	84-X	$7.95	
	SELF-MANAGEMENT			
	Attitude: Your Most Priceless Possession-Revised	011-6	$7.95	
	Personal Time Management	22-X	$7.95	
	Successful Self-Management	26-2	$7.95	
	Balancing Home And Career—Revised	035-3	$7.95	
	Developing Positive Assertiveness	38-6	$7.95	
	The Telephone And Time Management	53-X	$7.95	
	Memory Skills In Business	56-4	$7.95	
	Developing Self-Esteem	66-1	$7.95	
	Creativity In Business	67-X	$7.95	
	Managing Personal Change	74-2	$7.95	
	Stop Procrastinating: Get To Work!	88-2	$7.95	
	CUSTOMER SERVICE/SALES TRAINING			
	Sales Training Basics—Revised	02-5	$7.95	
	Restaurant Server's Guide—Revised	08-4	$7.95	
	Telephone Courtesy And Customer Service	18-1	$7.95	
	Effective Sales Management	031-0	$7.95	
	Professional Selling	42-4	$7.95	
	Customer Satisfaction	57-2	$7.95	
	Telemarketing Basics	60-2	$7.95	
	Calming Upset Customers	65-3	$7.95	
	Quality At Work	72-6	$7.95	
	Managing Quality Customer Service	83-1	$7.95	
	Quality Customer Service—Revised	95-5	$7.95	
	SMALL BUSINESS AND FINANCIAL PLANNING			
	Understanding Financial Statements	022-1	$7.95	
	Marketing Your Consulting Or Professional Services	40-8	$7.95	

THE FIFTY-MINUTE SERIES (Continued)

Quantity	Title	Code #	Price	Amount
	SMALL BUSINESS AND FINANCIAL PLANNING (CONTINUED)			
	Starting Your New Business	44-0	$7.95	
	Personal Financial Fitness—Revised	89-0	$7.95	
	Financial Planning With Employee Benefits	90-4	$7.95	
	BASIC LEARNING SKILLS			
	Returning To Learning: Getting Your G.E.D.	002-7	$7.95	
	Study Skills Strategies—Revised	05-X	$7.95	
	The College Experience	007-8	$7.95	
	Basic Business Math	024-8	$7.95	
	Becoming An Effective Tutor	028-0	$7.95	
	CAREER PLANNING			
	Career Discovery	07-6	$7.95	
	Effective Networking	030-2	$7.95	
	Preparing for Your Interview	033-7	$7.95	
	Plan B: Protecting Your Career	48-3	$7.95	
	I Got the Job!	59-9	$7.95	
	RETIREMENT			
	Personal Financial Fitness—Revised	89-0	$7.95	
	Financial Planning With Employee Benefits	90-4	$7.95	

OTHER CRISP INC. BOOKS

Quantity	Title	Code #	Price	Amount
	Desktop Publishing	001-9	$ 7.95	
	Stepping Up To Supervisor	11-8	$13.95	
	The Unfinished Business Of Living: Helping Aging Parents	19-X	$12.95	
	Managing Performance	23-7	$19.95	
	Be True To Your Future: A Guide To Life Planning	47-5	$13.95	
	Up Your Productivity	49-1	$10.95	
	Comfort Zones: Planning Your Future 2/e	73-4	$13.95	
	Copyediting 2/e	94-7	$18.95	
	Recharge Your Career	027-2	$12.95	
	Practical Time Management	275-4	$13.95	

VIDEO TITLE*

Quantity	Video Title*	Code #	Preview	Purchase	Amount
	Attitude: Your Most Priceless Possession	012-4	$25.00	$395.00	
	Quality Customer Service	013-2	$25.00	$395.00	
	Team Building	014-2	$25.00	$395.00	
	Job Performance & Chemical Dependency	015-9	$25.00	$395.00	
	Better Business Writing	016-7	$25.00	$395.00	
	Comfort Zones	025-6	$25.00	$395.00	
	Creativity in Business	036-1	$25.00	$395.00	
	Motivating at Work	037-X	$25.00	$395.00	
	Calming Upset Customers	040-X	$25.00	$395.00	
	Balancing Home and Career	048-5	$25.00	$395.00	
	Stress and Mental Fitness	049-3	$25.00	$395.00	

(*Note: All tapes are VHS format. Video package includes five books and a Leader's Guide.)

THE FIFTY-MINUTE SERIES
(Continued)

	Amount
Total Books	
Less Discount (5 or more different books 20% sampler)	
Total Videos	
Less Discount (purchase of 3 or more videos earn 20%)	
Shipping ($3.50 per video, $.50 per book)	
California Tax (California residents add 7%)	
TOTAL	

☐ Send volume discount information.

☐ Please charge the following credit card

☐ Please send me a catalog.

☐ Mastercard ☐ VISA ☐ AMEX

Account No. _____ Name (as appears on card) _____

Ship to: _____ Bill to: _____

_____ _____

_____ _____

_____ _____

Phone number: _____ P.O. # _____

All orders except those with a P.O.# must be prepaid.
For more information Call (415) 949-4888 or FAX (415) 949-1610.

BUSINESS REPLY

FIRST CLASS   PERMIT NO. 884   LOS ALTOS, CA

POSTAGE WILL BE PAID BY ADDRESSEE

Crisp Publications, Inc.
95 First Street
Los Altos, CA 94022

NO POSTAGE
NECESSARY
IF MAILED
IN THE
UNITED STATES

17402936